The Story of Me

Brian Arleth

Series Editor • Mark Pearcy

Contents

3	Learning About Our Past
4	South Korea: The Hanbok Tradition
8	Ethiopia: The Coffee Tradition
12	Brazil: The Capoeira Tradition
14	Traditions and You
16	Glossary/Index

Learning About Our Past

Every person has a story. How do you learn your story? Traditions can help. A tradition happens many times. It is passed down from person to person. Traditions can teach you about your **ancestry**.

South Korea, Ethiopia, and Brazil have traditions. Keep reading to learn more.

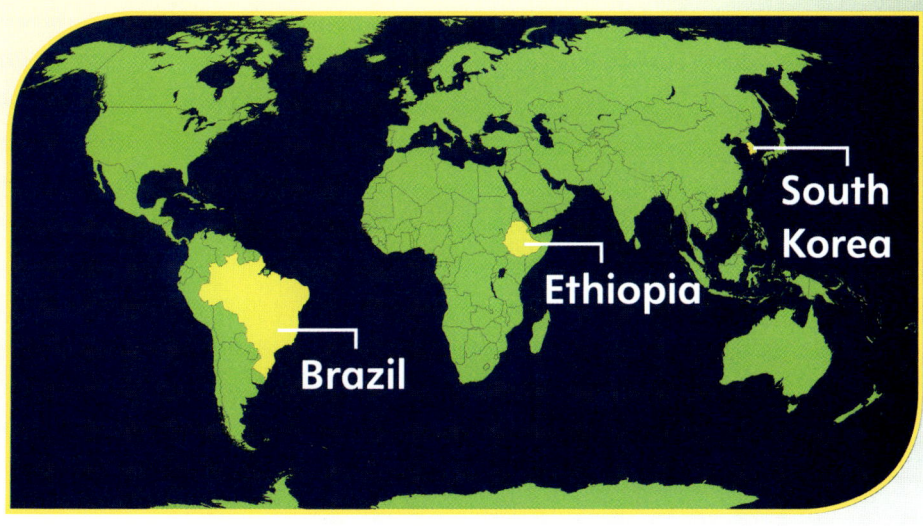

South Korea: The Hanbok Tradition

South Korea has a tradition called hanbok. Hanbok is clothing.

Hanbok can have many colors.

In the past, people wore hanbok every day. Today, people wear it on special days.

People sometimes wear hanbok at weddings.

An E-mail From South Korea

To: Mom and Dad

From: Brian

Subject: My New Clothes

Hi Mom and Dad!

Last weekend, I was part of a Korean holiday. It was like Thanksgiving. It was a harvest festival.

I went to a village with my Korean friend. We **celebrated** the harvest.

I wore hanbok. I wore a jacket and pants. I liked wearing these clothes. I liked the bright colors.

Everyone in my friend's family wore hanbok. This tradition brought people together.

I will talk to you soon.

Love,

Brian

Games and music are part of this holiday.

Ethiopia: The Coffee Tradition

There are different foods and drinks around the world.

People in Ethiopia have coffee **ceremonies.** These events happen in people's homes.

Coffee ceremonies can be very long.

Coffee is important in Ethiopia. It was most likely **invented** there.

One story says that a farmer's goats ate some plants. Then the goats were full of energy. Later, people made a drink with the beans from the plants. They called it coffee.

An E-mail From Ethiopia

To: Mom and Dad

From: Brian

Subject: Smell the Coffee

Hi Mom and Dad!

Yesterday, I saw a coffee ceremony. A woman roasted coffee beans. Then she crushed the beans.

People gathered. The woman put the beans in a pot of water. Then she poured everyone a drink. This brought people together.

I will bring home some coffee beans for you.

Your son,

Brian

For Your Information

Some say the third cup of coffee is lucky.

Brazil:
The Capoeira Tradition

Many people like to play games. Playing games can help people remember their past.

Capoeira (cap-oh-WAY-ra) is a tradition from Brazil. It is a game. The players look as if they are fighting.

Capoeira is an old tradition. It helps people from Brazil to stay active. It helps them remember their roots, too.

An E-mail From Brazil

To: Mom and Dad

From: Brian

Subject: Playing in Brazil

Hi Mom and Dad!

Today, I went to a restaurant. I saw some men stand in a circle. Then two men started to play a game of capoeira.

Capoeira looks hard! I want to try it, though. Can I take a few lessons?

Your son,

Brian

Traditions and You

Traditions help us learn about others. They help us remember our past. They make us feel that we **belong**.

Are there any traditions in your story? Think of a new tradition. What is important to your family? Choose one thing. Then celebrate it!

Glossary

ancestry: relatives who are older than a person's grandparents

belong: to fit in with others

celebrate: to do something fun to show an event is special

ceremony: a specific action or set of actions that is carried out according to tradition

invent: to create or design for the first time

Index

Brazil, 3, 12–13
capoeira, 12–13
coffee, 8–11
Ethiopia, 3, 8–10

hanbok, 4–5, 7
South Korea, 3–4, 6
Thanksgiving, 6